"Leave the gun. Take the cannoli"

—*The Godfather*

MAGRITTE'S MISSING MURALS

Insomniac Episodes

JOSEPH D. REICH

© 2017 by Joseph D. Reich
Book design © 2017 by Sagging Meniscus Press

All Rights Reserved.

Printed in the United States of America.
Set in Mrs Eaves XL with LaTeX.

ISBN: 978-1-944697-36-5 (paperback)
ISBN: 978-1-944697-37-2 (ebook)
Library of Congress Control Number: 2017931957

Sagging Meniscus Press
web: http://www.saggingmeniscus.com/
email: info@saggingmeniscus.com

Magritte's

Missing

Murals

1.

Just a ticking clock in a white birch forest
not positive in the form of the moon or sun

2.

A ship in a bottle in an empty room
moving towards the monstrous
doom of the wave of a tsunami

3.

Downpour falling from an ominous cloud
coming down in teardrops of a Coke bottle

4.

A 24-hour boxcar diner teetering off a cliff
on the edge of a precipice about to slip

5.

A lighthouse which just projects
darkness in a land of brightness

6.

A drive-in which shows very vivid porno
while its startled patrons sit in awe
prim and proper with perfect
etiquette propped in cars

7.

A crow who simply hitches on the side of
the road while a salesman in the form of
roadkill, briefcase and all, head down,
downtrodden, with bloody guts and
internal organs splattered all over

8.

A gorgeous voluptuous timid woman
holding up and pointing a gun at some
bandit-magician tied down to the tracks

9.

A superhero only able to rip off half
his shirt, passed-out, muted, coiled
in the phone booth in his striped
Madison Avenue business suit

10.

Prostitutes and stray dogs wash
themselves off under cascades of
flooding water roaring out of hydrants

11.

An ole time boxer sweeping some alley
focused, diligent in the desolate shadows
tucked in a corner of dark dingy buildings

12.

A man laid-out spread-eagle
on the phlebotomist table
looking like Jesus

13.

A petrified young naked woman
with tears in her eyes tied-down
to a chair with a burning blue
blazing guitar in the corner

14.

A sado-masochistic dominatrix in her
leather outfit with her whip and a frail
businessman in his suit on his knees
with a night table and lit lamp and
a glass of water and spectacles in
the middle of one of those rings
at the circus and a whole crowd of
docile spectators with blindfolds on

15.

Those perfectly-sculpted cliff divers in their
ole time bathing suits standing side by side
on the edge about to jump off and above
them a clothesline with a tightrope walker
and swinging laundry and looking down
below into some gorge there is a barker
with his bullhorn, strong man from the
circus lifting barbells, a fire swallower
swallowing fire, a clown and a juggler

16.

A schizophrenic crossing guard
with his elastic expressions
simply standing with his
stop sign slouched down
to his ankles beneath a
apple tree having shed
a ring of fiery leaves

17.

Two gigantic eggs simultaneously
sitting side by side with slight cracks
in their backs in front of the ocean
from the viewpoint of whitewashed
decaying crumbling Felliniesque buildings
in some sparse desert set back from shore

18.

Tugs pushing in pristine statues
of mythological gods through
the fog of a shattered skyline

19.

Rockettes in their top hats and tails
with leotards on in a long line kicking
their legs at the top of a waterfall
followed by the exact same rows
of synchronized monochromatic
girls and when they all reach
the bottom loops around
like a reel-to-reel projector

20.

Geeks and carnival freaks disheveled and
disoriented being led out in klutzy couples
from caravans like a madman Noah's Ark

21.

A brilliant Cubist form deconstructed
whose simple spare geometric shapes
have fallen to the floor with a bloody
knife and gun or maybe just a lasso

22.

A firing squad lined up with blindfolds
on smoking cigarettes each one tied-up
with rope while the convict sits back
in his easy chair reading the paper with
a side table and a lamp on and dog asleep
on the floor leaned up against a brick wall

23.

Some priest at a deathbed
with back hunched over
holding a bible wearing
women's underwear

24.

Cinderella in her mascara and blush
with her tiara and pumps and legs
spread open giving birth to 7 punks.

She's sick of giving up, accepting her
fate, and being stepped on, while in real time
those red flashing lights from the ambulance
show up to deliver them all to the orphanage

25.

Melancholia as always falls in
the regions of Louisiana, Biloxi,
Oklahoma, Southern Illinois, and
Iowa. When there's nothing left to live
for the ballerina and bride and groom
ditch and escape their snow globes.
They have been betrayed and under-
estimated way too many times before
by those they thought they loved.
Romantic boys from The Bible Belt
show up with dusty roses from their
bombshelters for girls they grew up
with, while some affluent attention-
seeking daughter with a sexual-identity
disorder sweeps in religiously late in her
powder-blue debutante gown pouting once
more that nothing anymore revolves around her

26.

A monster asleep beneath the bed
while up on top just a frosty bottle
of milk with a plate full of cookies

27.

Martha Washington knitting a flag
on a porch with her ankles tied to
the rocking chair and mischievous
rambunctious boys sniffing model
glue with gigantic smokestacks
puffing plumes over distant roofs

28.

Crows sitting perched atop
a gigantic keyhole with an
overcast tenebrous sky in back

29.

Some magician in costume
bent over a top hat only to see
the lid to the bottom eaten-out

30.

a.

Old art critics gathered around
a Fall foliage scene with mountains
and a barn and covered bridge in
a picture frame noticing a couple
of the pieces to the puzzle missing

b.

Same Fall foliage scene turning out
the world exists within a gigantic
bubblegum machine

c.

Same Fall foliage scene turning out
the world's a gigantic boy hunched
over with magnifying glass and all
those gorgeous trees on fire

d.

A very beautiful spare solitary still life
picture of a country home with colorful
autumn leaves fallen all around and a wood
pile in flames beneath the light of the moon

31.

A brother and sister from the carnival
just standing there holding hands, svelte, frail
with pained smiles in the middle of a hail storm

32.

The skeleton
stems & petals
of dried-up flowers
in the vase on the
bathroom windowsill
like a little kid who
stands like a milk
bottle in a milk
box with a smile
on the porch
waiting to get
picked up . . .

33.

A red rose leans over
sulking over a dark toilet
A red rose sneaks peeks
through a splintered keyhole
A red rose actively
engulfs the shadows
A red rose stoned in the splendor
of squalor of a magnificent ghetto
A red rose lying on top of a
lily-white ivory blood-stained pillow
A red rose blooming miraculously
in the middle of a snowstorm
against an ancient brick wall
A red rose giving birth to a red rose
giving birth to a red rose giving birth
to a red rose until all that's left
is a tiny white egg up on top of
a sill in the middle of a garden
A line of red roses pinned to a
clothesline raining red raindrops

A giant red rose being pushed
by mini tugs into muggy harbor
A red rose are all those glowing
red lights on the side of a horse
caravan dragging them through
the misty rainy evening to their
final holy and solemn destiny
A reflection of a red rose
in the switchblade of a ghost
A gargantuan red rose with
a flamenco dancer in its jaws
A monkey stealthily tugging
a bouquet of red roses from
a dewy table in downtown
Andalucía down an alley
of cobblestone to the
sparkling ocean
A Mafioso in dark dead man's
suit with hands behind his back
one holding a gun
one holding a red rose

A red rose hanging from a noose
from the middle of the ceiling
A red rose in the outstretched palm
of a gorgeous naked red-haired girl
with tormented eyes shut closed
in the middle of her bed
A red rose hysterically weeping
on the floor of a deathbed
A red rose like a mood of forget
me not blue dose of medicine
sweet sangria humbleness
reflection and false etiquette
A gigantic red rose discovered
on top of the mountain instead
of a flashing red radio antenna
A schoolyard fence lined with
red roses and a long bench full
of seductive school girls with
tricks up their sleeves in parochial
school dresses watching wild innocent
boys fight in the mud for their honor
framed for just this time and moment

A red rose planted next to a sign
next to a cathedral which reads
the next time for confession
A blinking red rose in the midnight
window with a view of a ballerina's
dripping brassieres on the bending
clothesline, the alchy landlord's
vegetable garden, and Brooklyn
Shipyard when the bells and foghorns
like a limerick and lullaby come
sweeping over the town, tucking
in those tongue-tied and turned-out
A red rose growing up the hollow
mouth of a fast-food clown
A red rose by any other name
is a red rose is a red rose
is a read rows of skulls
and bones of how civilization
began alongside the overflowing
Nile which nourished its soil while
also ended in the illusion of its grandeur
until all that stands is a final tourist taking

films from a smart phone for all his
monochromatic cloned idiot friends
A red rose whispers sweet nothings
and breathes and bends and pretends
A home blooms from the basement
of a red rose from the subterranean
bones and fear of the unknown

34.

The image of the human cannonball sitting at the head
of the supper table with his human cannonball children
and human cannonball wife who is naturally charming
and sympathetic and supportive and ironically
something of a neat freak and germophobe

35.

A map of The United States
of America colored in with
different shades of crayons
instead of those mountains
and rivers and tributaries
each different region
exhibiting a different
phenomenon like
wildfires due to
global warming,
rivers rising,
rivers drying,
highest murder rate,
highest suicide rate,
highest bullying rate,
highest intimidation rate
due to jocks/cheerleading,
highest real estate rates
which would include

homes and renting
and condos,
most malls,
most stripmalls,
best schools,
best carnivals,
highest rate of kkk,
highest opiate rate . . .

36.

A rushing rattling train and within
its windowpanes a sun sinking over
the geometric silhouetted roofs of
suburban homes while faceless
businessmen stand as straight
as trees in a forest and the flesh
of naked women lie like rivers
at their toes on the platform

37.

These selfsame soulless salesmen
following their inky shadows home
over waterfalls through vacant villages
through the distant image of boys
looking down from industrial
windows with bars in them

38.

Smokestacks on the shoulders
of a smoking factory on a
frozen lake juxtaposed by
the image of busy bundled-up
ice fishermen staked at its radius

39.

A whole mess of bluebirds
beating out a brick dingy chimney
up into a blazing bright red evening

40.

The pied piper bound and gagged
locked-up in a cage while a very tall
thin man sits on a simple school chair
blowing a harmonica and the children
from the town crawling out the valley
and alley and cave of the mountain

41.

A secret tavern set back in the bourgeois
forest no one really knows about meant
for just men and their mistresses and the
flamboyant cross dresser cabaret singer
and his accompanist with feasts of rabbit
and sweetbreads and soufflés and brandy
where across the midnight lake is a stone
tower which has been there for ages and
all you hear are the primal ceremonies
of deaf children howling like wild
animals beneath the constellations

42.

A mansion set back in the mountains
which has been passed down from generation to generation where no one has
ever really seen the residents just the ghost
stories and gossip and rumors of the master
who used to be like some young muscular
mythological god who would just naturally
seduce and turn on the rich girls from old
money visiting from the city during the heat
of the summer and watch his every movement and make them swoon and shiver

43.

The blower of foghorns you never saw
whose sudden, brash, boisterous bellow
makes you feel right at home right at the
core of folklore like he was right next door
but also some half-crazed criminal scaring
the hell out of you, making you jump
straight out your skin, reigniting your
shattered soul and will not only welcome
and warn the foreign ships, but literally
shake and rattle the frosty lattices of the
village (the barrooms and bridges) which
will include mothers on a mission with
warm breads baking in the oven, drunk
uncles, incestuous cousins, and young
forbidden lovers who aren't supposed to
see each other, leaving everything open
to the imagination, throbbing and tender

44.

Wild intoxicated girls dancing through
the pockmarked mists after liberating
redemptive nights of karaokeing
while in more ways than not
having worked the nightshift

45.

At the very posh resort & spa
way up on top the mountain
the shutters are on fire while
the young polite doormen
with wooden expressions
just stand there waiting
to usher in the conventions
of wives who have escaped
their husbands and while also
under the influence test to see
if their seductions still working
and viewed as attractive but
more in a herd-like mentality
on out-of-work actors forced
to have to swallow their pride,
act flattered, and keep it all inside
while these vulgar and obscene pathetic
performances are made to keep them alive

46.

Once you get off the highway it naturally feeds
into a scenic poverty-stricken depressed little town
where the main drag runs past an old burntdown
insane asylum, creamery, crematorium, family-
owned gravestones, next door to a boxcar diner,
a neat and tidy motel and ancient, nostalgic movie
theater; miniature golf and eventually a hamburger
stand whose beacon has always helped to measure
the mad passing of seasons; they got something for
everyone and when you continue on a little further
through some token, eternal, blinking traffic light on
the corner of the cobblestone alley which extends
to the keyhole of the curtain of the mountains, you
get to the infamous boarding school with undulating
lawns where you never see a living, breathing soul
(which gives it that existential yet fictional feel) right
next to the country club and spa and yes, suppose
there is that classic rock & roll song—"got to go
through hell before you get to heaven" but in this

case, not so sure, while ironically on this side of
the tracks, the affluent side, if you only knew
what really went on behind closed doors; the
fine line and gorge between fact and folklore

47.

The family physician with his stethoscope
the stud gynecologist and seductive hygienists
float around the foggy fish bowl while the monster
from beneath the bed with groggy expressions
and steamed-up bifocals plays the role of hotel
clerk with a sign in front of him which simply reads
Vacanct, a creaky postcard carousel of haunted photos,
vase of plastic flowers, and instead of that required fire
extinguisher, a mask and tube and tank of nitrous oxide

48.

A dusty and defeated, dirty old man
most likely a salesman, peeking through
a peephole during his lunch hour in Time
Square only to glimpse the surprising image
of an animated, glossy Harlequin cover of
some big, muscular, stud-gigolo, grasping
onto the torso of his long-lost romantic lover

49.

Here come the explorers
from beneath the bridge
having spent a whole
lifetime under there
no longer
a fear
of success
no longer
a fear
of failure
just stoically
standing there
on the edge
of barges
like some mock
Buddha madmen
waving with pigeons
on their shoulders proud
long-lost true-blue sailors

50.

He hangs over the side of his folded
origami boat, punch-drunk, paper-cut
puking into the decadent fountain of
tourists and aristocrats, who act aloof
and arrogant and treat everyone like a
possession, leaving him tongue-tied,
trembling, not so innocent anymore
and desperately alone, now just a
stoned stowaway to an unfamiliar
hollowed-out, hurt, and holy soul

51.

The back of a box of cereal
reflecting the opposite image
of some boy looking out
with his bowl of cereal
and spoon to the moon

52.

Some frail old man in his pastel pajamas
climbing up a ladder into the window
lit on fire into an empty spare room
which looks like a perfectly manicured back-
yard with hedges and a beaming bright sun

53.

An old woman getting engulfed
and swallowed with her head up
the mouth of a swan by the pond

54.

A candidate with his back to the camera
at one of those town hall meetings
flashing a team of seething feminists

55.

Two families squaring off standing across
from each other in a game show while
right in the middle is a bloody battle
between bold brave soldiers of
complete horror and carnage

56.

Some macho heroic Lone Ranger character
still on his horse with his mask on holding
up a set of toll booths with no one in them

57.

A sexless mother with her ballerina
glaring at some bleary-eyed laborer
brow-beaten at the hamburger stand

58.

A portrait from the back while bent over
showing the snatch or panties wedged
up the sweet crack of some gorgeous
voluptuous female dictator waving
passionately from her tiny bath-
room window while all you see
are the buzzing bobbing tops of
the mops of men cheering crazily

59.

A simple spare portrait
of a stunning aloof lifeguard
to die for with head perched
high up in the clouds sitting
way atop a lookout like some
queen on her throne while right
behind her lies a long stretch of
splashed-out bushy mountains

60.

Bare mountains with tree stumps up
and down them and a procession
of caskets moving downriver

61.

A simple and spare shadowy film-noir
bedroom with bulletholes shot through
and the eyes of a voyeur peeking
through with body parts in ruins

62.

A sparse and clean empty room
with a gorgeous alabaster naked girl
with her heart-shaped buttocks and just
a stethoscope dangling around her shoulders

63.

Aristocratic lakes and mountains
which come down upside-down
over the rising sun of verandas

64.

Just one perfectly-sculpted gigolo
along shore opening up all the
striped beach chairs early
in the morning, hosing them
down around some stranded
older woman, who appears
lost and brooding, bathing
buck-naked, and seeming
engaged in some existential
self-conscious, weird rebellion
hostile and passive-aggressive
from a past identity of seductive siren
to present day reality of seething savage

65.

The image of very aristocratic women putting on
their makeup in front of dressing room mirrors
before the tragedy of the Titanic and Hindenburg

while Rawshack and Heimlich Maneuver
get ready for the grand drag queen ball
all swingers in one form or another

66.

Freaks from the freakshow
very focused, diligent, driven,
and detail-oriented wash themselves off
by the ocean when the cruise ships come in

67.

One of those great big luxury liners
while in the portholes at the bottom
just highlighting the expressions
of wives looking out nihilistic
wondering and worried for
their loved ones out at sea
while just above you see
them in their very fancy
tuxedos waltzing nonchalantly
with young seductive ladies
and out on the captain's deck
a monkey with his accordion
looking out with binoculars

68.

Through the lens of a pair of binoculars
showing a close-up of some ancient
castle with Venetian blinds barely
open in windows making reverse
shadows and reflections

69.

An ancient tiny whitewashed cathedral
with a windy bell still in its thimble
gets dragged across a deep solid
frozen lake and placed within
the dense trees of an upside
down forest which separates
one side of the mystical
lake from the other

70.

A well-sculpted acrobat doing
a somersault backwards hanging
from twin nooses from the rafters

71.

Some poor man on his knees trying
desperately to bring back to life
and resuscitate one of those blow-
up Wise Men with a couple of them
already standing and idiot neighbors
surrounding him with sarcastic
and insensitive expressions

72.

A hoodlum whacking a nun
on the back of the butt
with a ruler all tied-up
and a blindfold on
letting out moans
of orgiastic pleasure

73.

That top hat image with his back
from the viewer in front of a lovely
whitewashed country home; a sort
of self-entitled bio-portrait of M.
tossing rocks very precisely at the
corners of windows trying to make
them smash a little and make it look
more atmospheric, solemn and haunted

74.

A garage all filled-up with bickering
neighbors while outside in the bizarre
fictional real world domestic pets
roam happily ever after around
pastel placid peaceful lawns

75.

Poor Jesus being crucified on his hands
and knees being followed down the alley
by some silly, harassing college coach
with a whistle and bullhorn (the running
of the bulls has been permanently postponed)
a matador getting his portrait drawn by
the king's son posing as a starving artist
looking forward to his days on death row,
the fortune teller with her shattered globe
smokes cigars stoically in a neon window
while her con-artist stepsons holler—
"you don't know what you're talking of!"
petty thieves peeking around the corner,
flamenco dancers, hustlers, Dolce Vita
daughters beneath umbrellas; miserable
fake aristocratic women going out of their
way to prove that everything and nothing
exists around them, like widows going
window shopping for wedding dresses

when the streetwalkers come out
below the street lamps at sunset,
pimps and priests and drag queens
return home bleary-eyed from the
meat market, the king of hearts
with his distant and damaged
look, oblivious, heartbroken
tossing pizza in the window,
college cheerleaders in short
skirts and sequins with million-dollar
smiles strutting their stuff for the blood-
thirsty savages at the dinner theater,
the poverty-stricken brother and sister
selling roses and newspapers, hitching
a ride on the back of the puppet master's
rickshaw, rundown, on-the-run from the law
a screen and slide projector
a staticky scoreboard up above

76.

Some man with a gun to his head
and out the other ear blooms
a bouquet of flowers

77.

A bowl of waxed fruit set in the middle
of some solitary table with chattering
teeth by its side and dentures
in an empty goblet of wine

78.

A skeleton from the closet suffocated
zipped-up in plastic-wrapped furniture

79.

Different stages of human growth
& development such as a kid
trying to impress his friends
spinning around in the dryer

When he gets older showing
the desire and arousal of
spying on naked sister
through the keyhole

A whole dresser drawer
of Barbie doll heads
snapped off them

A very tall slim man standing
straight as a pencil in his gray
dusty suit inside the shadowy
shelter of a grandfather clock

Last portrait of a pair of binoculars
simply dangling around a mailbox
as if somehow caught by the
neighbors across the block

80.

A used-car lot and signs for politicians
scattered beneath the mountain with an
active volcano literally blowing its top

81.

A whole herd of old timers in pastel
ten-gallons clomping out the square
dance like a procession of robots
down the creaky stairs through
the tourist shop disappearing
in thin air to the trailer park
to their mansions in the dust

82.

A wilted window
behind a vase of flowers
with the petals shattered

83.

A storming forest
with fireflies flashing right
over the silhouette of treetops

84.

With your insomnia you dream of being
a very thin man and slipping between
your dreams and nightmares, your
perseverating like a prayer; think
of that image of that man inching
very cautiously and precariously
to center ring with his whip and
his chair, who was that again?
The lion tamer? The psychotic
elephant trainer? How weird
and you wonder what exactly
that is used for, but guess if
it works like yeast to bread

The man who likes to take risks
and chances, does he really
like to or is he just desperate?

Joseph Reich is a social worker and displaced New Yorker who lives with his wife and eleven-year-old son up in the high mountains of Vermont. He has been published in a wide variety of eclectic literary journals both here and abroad, and been nominated six times for The Pushcart Prize.

OTHER BOOKS BY JOSEPH D. REICH

A Different Sort Of Distance (Skive Magazine Press, 2010)
If I Told You To Jump Off The Brooklyn Bridge (Flutter Press, 2010)
Pain Diary: Working Methadone & The Life & Times Of The Man Sawed In Half
   (Brick Road Poetry Press, 2010)
Drugstore Sushi (Thunderclap Press, 2010)
Escaping Shangrila (Punkin Press, 2011)
The Derivation of Cowboys and Indians (Fomite Press, 2012)
The Housing Market: a comfortable place to jump off the end of the world
   (Fomite Press, 2013)
The Hole That Runs Through Utopia (Fomite Press, 2014)
*Taking The Fifth And Running With It: A Psychological Guide for the Hard of Hearing
   and Blind* (Broadstone Books, 2015)
Connecting the Dots to Shangrila: A Postmodern Cultural History of America
   (Fomite Press, 2016)
The Rituals of Mummification (Sagging Meniscus, 2016)